The Wright Brothers

by Kitty Shea

Compass Point Early Biographies

Content Adviser: Roger E. Bilstein, Ph.D., Professor of History Emeritus,
University of Houston-Clear Lake, Houston, Texas

Reading Adviser: Susan Kesselring, M.A., Literacy Educator,
Rosemount-Apple Valley-Eagan (Minnesota) School District

COMPASS POINT BOOKS
MINNEAPOLIS, MINNESOTA

Compass Point Books
3109 West 50th Street, #115
Minneapolis, MN 55410

Visit Compass Point Books on the Internet at *www.compasspointbooks.com*
or e-mail your request to *custserv@compasspointbooks.com*

Photographs ©: From the Historical and Interpretive Collections of The Franklin Institute, Inc.,
Philadelphia, PA, cover; Library of Congress, cover background, 10; Courtesy of Special Collections
and Archives, Wright State University, 4, 6 (all), 8, 9, 11, 14, 15, 17, 19, 22, 24; Corbis, 5;
Hulton/Archive by Getty Images, 7, 12, 16, 26; Stockbyte, 13; From the Historical and Interpretive
Collections of The Franklin Institute, Inc., Philadelphia, PA, photograph by Charles Penniman, 18;
NASA, 20, 23; PhotoDisc, 25; George Hall/Corbis, 27.

Creative Director: Terri Foley
Managing Editor: Catherine Neitge
Editor: Brenda Haugen
Photo Researcher: Svetlana Zhurkina
Designer/Page production: Bradfordesign, Inc./Jaime Martens
Educational Consultant: Diane Smolinski

Library of Congress Cataloging-in-Publication Data
Shea, Kitty.
The Wright brothers / by Kitty Shea.
p. cm. — (Compass Point early biographies)
Includes bibliographical references and index.
ISBN 0-7565-0791-X (hardcover)
1. Wright, Orville, 1871-1948—Juvenile literature. 2. Wright, Wilbur, 1867-1912—
Juvenile literature. 3. Aeronautics—United States—Biography—Juvenile literature.
4. Inventors—United States—Biography—Juvenile literature. I. Title. II. Series.
TL540.W7S43 2004
629.13'0092'273—dc22   2004005689

Table of Contents

A Dream That People Could Fly 5

Growing Up 6

Working Together 10

Building Gliders 12

Kitty Hawk 14

Testing Wings 16

Success! 18

More Work to Do 21

An Important Invention 25

Important Dates in the Lives
of Wilbur and Orville Wright 28

Glossary 29

Did You Know? 30

Want to Know More? 31

Index 32

NOTE: In this book, words that are defined in the glossary are in **bold** *the first time they appear in the text.*

A Dream That People Could Fly

Before Wilbur and Orville Wright came along, there had been all sorts of flying machines. None of these machines could be controlled by a pilot and flown safely, however. Many felt it was crazy for people to think they could fly.

French plane with many wings

The Wright brothers proved it could be done. After many tries, the brothers built an airplane that was run by an engine and steered by a pilot. The Wright brothers believed in their dream and made it come true.

This is the story of the Wright brothers.

◀ Wilbur (left) and Orville Wright

Growing Up

Wilbur and Orville Wright were always interested in mechanics, or how things work. As children, the brothers earned money by selling toys they had created. They also were interested in flying. Orville made and sold kites to neighborhood children.

Wilbur around age 13

Orville around age 10

Orville (third from right) and Wilbur (second from right) stand with some members of their family in 1903.

Wilbur Wright was born April 16, 1867. Orville arrived four years later on August 19, 1871. They had two older brothers and one younger sister.

The Wright family
moved a lot before
settling in Dayton,
Ohio. Wilbur and
Orville's father,
Milton, was a
Protestant church
bishop. He taught
his children to be
honest and fair. Their
mother, Susan, showed

Susan Koerner Wright

them how to work with their hands. She was
good at fixing and building things. She even
made toys for her children.

When Wilbur was 11 years old and Orville was 7, their father gave them a toy helicopter. A rubber band sprang the helicopter into the air. It made the Wright brothers want to fly, too.

Young Wilbur and Orville decided to make their own helicopter. They copied the toy piece by piece but made theirs bigger. Their helicopter didn't work as well as the toy one.

Bishop Milton Wright

Working Together

Wilbur finished high school, but the family moved before he could get his **diploma.** Orville left school to run a print shop and publish a newspaper.

Edwin H. Sines works in Orville's print shop. Along with working for the Wright brothers, Sines was also their neighbor.

He asked Wilbur to work with him.

The two brothers worked, lived, and played together. They were interested in some of the same things, but they were different from one another, too. Wilbur liked to read and think. Orville was always working on projects.

The Wright brothers' ➤ home in Dayton, Ohio

In 1892, Wilbur and Orville opened a bike shop in Dayton. They fixed, sold, and built bicycles. When business was slow, the brothers read books about flying.

Building Gliders

Wilbur and Orville built huge kites and **gliders** to learn about flying. Other inventors had gotten gliders to fly. The problem was controlling the gliders once they were in the air.

An eagle gets ready to land. The Wright brothers studied bird movements.

Wilbur and Orville studied birds in flight to get ideas for controlling their gliders.

But they still had many questions. What would power a glider through the sky? How could a pilot control where the glider flew? The Wright brothers knew these were the secrets to making a machine that could fly.

German inventor Otto Lilienthal flies from a hill in Berlin in 1896.

Kitty Hawk

In 1900, Wilbur and Orville made a double-decker glider. Their glider was made of wood, wire, and fabric. The brothers took the glider to a fishing village called Kitty Hawk in

North Carolina to see how it would fly.

Wilbur cleans a pan by using sand.

Orville and Wilbur camped on the beach near Kitty Hawk, but it was not a vacation. The weather was cold, and sand blew everywhere.

The strong winds near Kitty Hawk helped the Wright brothers launch their glider. The sand dunes softened its landings. Orville and Wilbur wanted to control the wings of their glider like a bird controls its wings. But something wasn't working right.

◀ Orville and Wilbur test a glider at Kill Devil Hills near Kitty Hawk.

Testing Wings

Back at their bike shop, Wilbur and Orville did lots of experiments. They needed to know more about wings.

The Wright brothers used a **wind tunnel** to test the wings of their model gliders. This helped them see what effects air would have on the wings. They tested more than 200 different wing types.

The wind tunnel the Wright brothers used is at the Smithsonian Institution in Washington, D.C.

Friend Dan Tate helps Wilbur Wright test the Wright 1902 glider at Kill Devil Hills.

Year after year, the Wright brothers returned to Kitty Hawk. They brought new and better gliders. Along with an **elevator,** they added a **rudder** to the glider. They designed a **propeller** and an engine. And in 1903, they flew.

Success!

The day was December 17, 1903. The wind was icy cold. Wilbur and Orville were nervous. They had named their latest machine the *Flyer*. They really wanted it to fly.

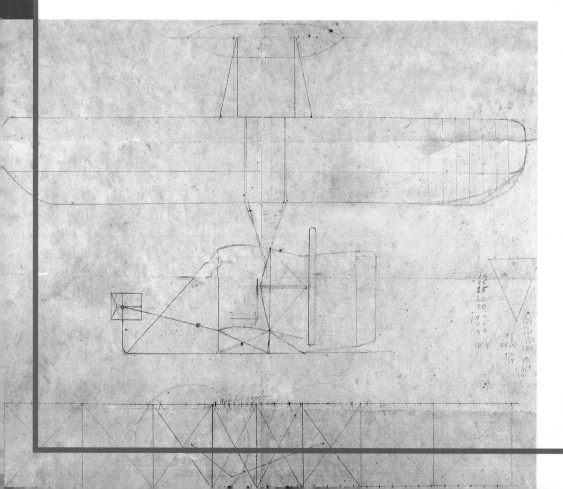

Orville puts the 1903 *Flyer* together inside a camp building at Kill Devil Hills.

The brothers had worked on their airplane in Kitty Hawk, but they launched it from nearby sand dunes called Kill Devil Hills.

◄ An early drawing of the *Flyer*

The Wright brothers get their machine to fly for the first time.

Orville got into the *Flyer*. Wilbur ran beside it as it took off. Orville flew for 12 seconds before landing safely. The *Flyer* had stayed in the air for about 120 feet (37 meters). Later that day, Wilbur flew for 59 seconds and went 852 feet (260 meters).

One of the men who had helped Wilbur and Orville that day ran into town yelling, "They done it! They done it!"

More Work to Do

The Wright brothers went home happy. They knew they couldn't sell the *Flyer* yet, though. It wouldn't be useful to the world until it could carry passengers or **cargo.**

Wilbur and Orville spent two more years improving their flying machine. They made new planes and worked on different motors. In 1905, they built a plane that could turn. It also could stay in the air for more than half an hour.

In all the times the Wright brothers flew, they only flew together once. Their father didn't want them to be in the same plane in case it crashed.

The Wright brothers got a **patent** for their plane in 1906. That meant people who wanted to make airplanes had to pay the Wright brothers to use their ideas.

The Wright brothers' 1906 patent for their flying machine

◀ Wilbur Wright sits in his Wright 1907 *Flyer* near Le Mans, France, in August 1908.

People make airplanes in the general assembly department at the
Wright Company in 1911.

In 1909, Wilbur and Orville opened
the Wright Company to make airplanes and
train pilots.

An Important Invention

In 1912, Wilbur died of a disease called typhoid fever at age 45. Orville lived to be 76 years old. The brothers never knew their **invention**

The Wright Brothers National Memorial in Manteo, North Carolina

would lead to the creation of planes that could fly faster than the speed of sound.

Today's airplanes still use the Wright brothers' basic ideas. Because of Wilbur and Orville, we can travel the skies.

An airplane of today

◀ Orville compares his biplane model with a
model of an airplane made in the 1940s.

Important Dates in the Lives of Wilbur and Orville Wright

1867	Wilbur born in Millville, Indiana, on April 16
1871	Orville born in Dayton, Ohio, on August 19
1878	Introduced to the idea of flight by a toy helicopter
1892	Opened a bicycle shop in Dayton, Ohio
1900	Began testing gliders at Kitty Hawk, North Carolina
1903	Performed the world's first controlled and powered flight in the *Flyer*
1905	Built the world's first practical airplane, the *Flyer III,* which could fly farther and longer than all of their previous flights combined
1906	Awarded a patent for a flying machine
1909	Formed the Wright Company to make airplanes
1912	Wilbur died in Dayton, Ohio, on May 30, at age 45
1915	Orville sold the Wright Company and retired
1948	Orville died in Dayton, Ohio, on January 30, at age 76
1948	1903 *Flyer* is put in the Smithsonian Institution, a museum in Washington, D.C.

Glossary

cargo—goods carried in a ship, an aircraft, or a vehicle

diploma—a certificate a person gets when he or she graduates from high school or college

elevator—a movable piece of an airplane that helps the pilot control whether the plane goes up or down

gliders—aircraft that use wind to fly instead of engines

invention—something new that a person thinks up and creates

patent—a document from the government that says an idea belongs to an inventor and is his or hers to use or sell

propeller—two or more twisted blades that spin to move an airplane forward

rudder—a movable piece on an airplane that allows the pilot to turn it left or right

wind tunnel—a passage through which air is blown to show how the air will affect an object, such as a model airplane

Did You Know?

- Wilbur and Orville's family and friends called them Will and Orv.

- Neither brother received a high school diploma or any formal training in engineering. In later years, however, they received a total of 15 honorary degrees from colleges and universities.

- Orville served as the Boy Scouts of America's adviser for the Aviation Merit Badge. More than 357,000 such badges were awarded to Scouts between 1911 and 2001.

- The brothers spent less than $1,000 building their gliders and the 1903 *Flyer*.

- In 1920, Orville became a member of the National Advisory Committee on Aeronautics. This committee later became the National Aeronautics and Space Administration (NASA). It is the U.S. government agency that oversees space travel.

- In 1969, when American Neil Armstrong became the first man to step on the moon, the astronaut was carrying a piece of fabric from the wing of the Wright brothers' 1903 *Flyer*.

Want to Know More?

At the Library

Carson, Mary Kay. *The Wright Brothers for Kids*. Chicago: Chicago Review Press, 2003.

Schaefer, Lola M. *The Wright Brothers*. Mankato, Minn.: Pebble Books, 2000.

Yolen, Jane. *My Brothers' Flying Machine: Wilbur, Orville, and Me*. New York: Little, Brown, 2003.

On the Web

For more information on the *Wright brothers,* use FactHound to track down Web sites related to this book.

1. Go to *www.facthound.com*
2. Type in a search word related to this book or this book ID: 075650791X.
3. Click on the *Fetch It* button.

Your trusty FactHound will fetch the best Web sites for you!

On the Road

Wright Brothers National Memorial

1401 National Park Drive

Manteo, NC 27954

252/441-7430

To see the hill from which the Wright brothers launched their glider flights, markers showing the distances they flew, and camp buildings reconstructed like those in which they stayed

Index

airplanes, *5,* 18–19, *18, 19,* 20, *20,* 21–24, *24,* 26, *26, 27*

birds, 13, *13,* 15

Dayton, Ohio, 8, 11, *11*

elevator, 17
engine, 17, 21
experiments, 16

Flyer aircraft, 18–19, *18, 19,* 20, *20,* 21, 22

gliders, 12, *12,* 13, 14–16, *14,* 17, *17*

Kill Devil Hills, North Carolina, *14, 17,* 19, *19*
kites, 6, 12
Kitty Hawk, North Carolina, 14–15, *14,* 17, 19

Lilienthal, Otto, *12*

patent, 23, *23*
pilots, 13, 24
print shop, 10, *10*
propeller, 17

rudder, 17

Sines, Edwin H., *10*
Smithsonian Institution, *16*

Tate, Dan, *17*
toy helicopter, 9

wind tunnel, 16, *16*
wings, 15, 16
Wright Brothers National Memorial, 25
Wright Company, 24, *24*
Wright, Milton (father), 8, 9, *9,* 21
Wright, Orville, 4, 6, 7, *14,* 19, 20, 26
  birth of, 7
  childhood of, 6, *6,* 9
  death of, 25
  education of, 10
Wright, Susan Koerner (mother), 8, *8*
Wright, Wilbur, 4, 6, 7, *14,* 15, 17, 20, 22
  birth of, 7
  childhood of, 6, *6,* 9
  death of, 25
  education of, 10

About the Author

Kitty Shea founded Ideas & Words in 1988 with the goal of following her curiosity into different writing disciplines and subject matter. She has since authored books for young readers, served as editor of home and travel magazines, edited cookbooks, and published hundreds of articles and essays. She has also taught in the journalism department of her alma mater, the University of St. Thomas in St. Paul, Minnesota.